General
Thomas Gage

British General

Colonial Leaders

Lord Baltimore
English Politician and Colonist

Benjamin Banneker
American Mathematician and Astronomer

Sir William Berkeley
Governor of Virginia

William Bradford
Governor of Plymouth Colony

Jonathan Edwards
Colonial Religious Leader

Benjamin Franklin
American Statesman, Scientist, and Writer

Anne Hutchinson
Religious Leader

Cotton Mather
Author, Clergyman, and Scholar

Increase Mather
Clergyman and Scholar

James Oglethorpe
Humanitarian and Soldier

William Penn
Founder of Democracy

Sir Walter Raleigh
English Explorer and Author

Caesar Rodney
American Patriot

John Smith
English Explorer and Colonist

Miles Standish
Plymouth Colony Leader

Peter Stuyvesant
Dutch Military Leader

George Whitefield
Clergyman and Scholar

Roger Williams
Founder of Rhode Island

John Winthrop
Politician and Statesman

John Peter Zenger
Free Press Advocate

Revolutionary War Leaders

John Adams
Second U.S. President

Samuel Adams
Patriot

Ethan Allen
Revolutionary Hero

Benedict Arnold
Traitor to the Cause

John Burgoyne
British General

George Rogers Clark
American General

Lord Cornwallis
British General

Thomas Gage
British General

King George III
English Monarch

Nathanael Greene
Military Leader

Nathan Hale
Revolutionary Hero

Alexander Hamilton
First U.S. Secretary of the Treasury

John Hancock
President of the Continental Congress

Patrick Henry
American Statesman and Speaker

William Howe
British General

John Jay
First Chief Justice of the Supreme Court

Thomas Jefferson
Author of the Declaration of Independence

John Paul Jones
Father of the U.S. Navy

Thaddeus Kosciuszko
Polish General and Patriot

Lafayette
French Freedom Fighter

James Madison
Father of the Constitution

Francis Marion
The Swamp Fox

James Monroe
American Statesman

Thomas Paine
Political Writer

Molly Pitcher
Heroine

Paul Revere
American Patriot

Betsy Ross
American Patriot

Baron Von Steuben
American General

George Washington
First U.S. President

Anthony Wayne
American General

Famous Figures of the Civil War Era

John Brown
Abolitionist

Jefferson Davis
Confederate President

Frederick Douglass
Abolitionist and Author

Stephen A. Douglas
Champion of the Union

David Farragut
Union Admiral

Ulysses S. Grant
Military Leader and President

Stonewall Jackson
Confederate General

Joseph E. Johnston
Confederate General

Robert E. Lee
Confederate General

Abraham Lincoln
Civil War President

George Gordon Meade
Union General

George McClellan
Union General

William Henry Seward
Senator and Statesman

Philip Sheridan
Union General

William Sherman
Union General

Edwin Stanton
Secretary of War

Harriet Beecher Stowe
Author of Uncle Tom's Cabin

James Ewell Brown Stuart
Confederate General

Sojourner Truth
Abolitionist, Suffragist, and Preacher

Harriet Tubman
Leader of the Underground Railroad

General
Thomas Gage

British General

Bonnie Hinman

Arthur M. Schlesinger, jr.
Senior Consulting Editor

Chelsea House Publishers

Philadelphia

CHELSEA HOUSE PUBLISHERS
Editor-in-Chief Sally Cheney
Director of Production Kim Shinners
Production Manager Pamela Loos
Art Director Sara Davis
Production Editor Diann Grasse

Staff for *GENERAL THOMAS GAGE*
Editor Sally Cheney
Associate Art Director Takeshi Takahashi
Series Design Keith Trego
Cover Design 21st Century Publishing and Communications, Inc.
Picture Researcher Jane Sanders
Layout 21st Century Publishing and Communications, Inc.

The Chelsea House World Wide Web address is
http://www.chelseahouse.com

First Printing
1 3 5 7 9 8 6 4 2

Library of Congress Cataloging-in-Publication Data

Hinman, Bonnie.
  General Thomas Gage / Bonnie Hinman.
     p. cm. — (Revolutionary War leaders)
  Includes bibliographical references and index.
  ISBN 0-7910-6384-4 (hc : alk. paper) — ISBN 0-7910-6385-2
  (pbk. : alk. paper)
    1. Gage, Thomas, 1721-1787—Juvenile literature. 2. Governors—
  Massachusetts—Biography—Juvenile literature. 3. Generals—
  Great Britain—Biography—Juvenile literature. 4. Colonial
  administrators—United States—Biography—Juvenile literature.
  5. United States—History—Revolution, 1775-1783—British forces
  —Juvenile literature. [1. Gage, Thomas, 1721-1787. 2. Generals.
  3. United States—History—Revolution, 1775-1783.] I. Title. II. Series.

F67.G34 H56 2001
973.3'3'092—dc21
[B]   2001028523

Publisher's Note: In Colonial and Revolutionary War America, there were no standard rules for spelling, punctuation, capitalization, or grammar. Some of the quotations that appear in the Colonial Leaders and Revolutionary War Leaders series come from original documents and letters written during this time in history. Original quotations reflect writing inconsistencies of the period.

Contents

The Thames River runs through London. The river was important to England as a source of drinking water and as a way to transport goods. Several bridges connect the northern and southern parts of London.

The Second Son

homas Gage came from an "unlucky" family, or at least that is how it must have seemed to him. The Gage family had come to Great Britain hundreds of years before Thomas Gage was born. Through all those years the Gages usually supported the losing side in a war or other disagreement.

Another problem for the Gages was their religion. The Gages were Roman Catholic in Britain in the 1700s when it was not popular to be a Catholic. Most people belonged to the Anglican Church, which was approved by the British government. The Gages were Roman Catholic until Thomas's father, Viscount

Gage, changed to the Anglican Church. (A viscount is a member of British peerage, ranking below an earl but above a baron.)

The use of horses was forbidden to anyone who was not loyal to the Anglican Church. One of Viscount Gage's friends, poet Alexander Pope, said that the Viscount became an Anglican in 1715 so he could keep horses. After he became an Anglican, Viscount Gage was elected to the House of Commons. He served in Parliament for 33 years.

Viscount Gage was known for his great love of gambling. His wife, Benedicta, loved to attend parties. The king at that time, George I, liked the Gages, and they were welcomed in London society.

Thomas was the second son born to the Gages. He was born in 1719 or early in 1720 (the exact date is not recorded). His older brother was William, and his younger sister was Theresa. They grew up at Highmeadow estate in Gloucestershire in southern England. It was a beautiful place to live. William and Thomas played together in the fields and woods near Highmeadow.

In January 1728 the brothers were sent to boarding school. Thomas was eight years old and his brother was ten at the time. They came home only for vacations.

The school Thomas and William went to was the well-known Westminster public school. A public school in England was different from one in the United States. "Public" actually meant that the school was private. Anyone could apply to a school but had to be accepted and pay tuition.

Thomas attended Westminster until 1736. William finished the year before. While there the brothers studied Latin, English literature, and other subjects. They also made many friends who would be useful to them when they were adults. Attending a famous school was very important to British upper-class families.

Not much is known about the years right after Thomas left Westminster. There is no record that he went to a university. He may have traveled through Europe. The "Grand Tour," as it was called, was often made by young Englishmen of his time.

Eventually Thomas had to choose a career. His father probably did not have a lot of money like some British nobles. William was the oldest son and would inherit the title of viscount and most of the money and property. There were only a few careers that were considered proper for a second son in the 1700s. Thomas could choose from the ministry, the law, government service, the army, or the navy.

Thomas chose the army. The British army had a system that let it get its officers from the upper classes of British citizens. Commissions in the army, which are what makes a man an officer, were for sale. Fathers, older brothers, or family friends arranged to purchase a commission from a soldier who had himself bought a higher-ranking commission. Thomas's first commission was purchased for him.

The young soldier also had to buy his own uniforms, tent, and other equipment. The money required to become an officer kept the poorer and lower-class British men from becoming officers. At that time it was considered proper that the higher-class citizens would be in charge of all others.

Thomas was first an ensign in the army. One of his jobs was to recruit new soldiers in Yorkshire. This was an easy job in pleasant surroundings. In 1741 Thomas purchased a commission as a lieutenant, and by 1743 he was a captain. In 1744 he went with the British troops to fight the French in Belgium. He took part in the Battle of Fontenoy, which was famous for how bloody it was. The British lost the battle.

Thomas also fought in the Battle of Culloden, which took place in Scotland. The rebellious Scottish clansmen fought bravely but found themselves overwhelmed by the British army. The moor at Culloden was littered with bodies of Scottish

British soldiers made a magnificent sight when they marched into an American town or city. The enlisted men wore brick-red coats while the officers wore brighter red or scarlet colored coats. They were soon nicknamed "redcoats" by the colonists. The trim on their coats and vests was different for each unit. One unit, the grenadiers, wore huge bearskin hats. The men chosen for the grenadiers were required to be tall. When a 12-inch or larger hat was added, these men looked like giants.

warriors. This time Thomas was on the winning side.

He served as an aide to the Duke of Albemarle. The Duke was the father of some of his school friends from Westminster. It was an honor to serve him, and Thomas did a good job. In 1748 a peace treaty was signed with France. Soon after that, Thomas transferred to another **regiment**, became a major, and eventually, a lieutenant colonel.

Great Britain was at peace for several years. Thomas was able to do other things besides be a soldier. He took trips to see his brother and went to Paris at least once. He also appeared at King George's court once or twice. Thomas was well liked by other soldiers who nicknamed him "Honest Tom."

Thomas made a short venture into politics. In 1753 his father was up for reelection in Tewksbury. He asked Thomas to run for another seat in the same **borough**. It was not unusual at that time for a military officer to run for the House of Commons. There was a dispute over the roads in the borough, which led to the defeat of both Gages. They

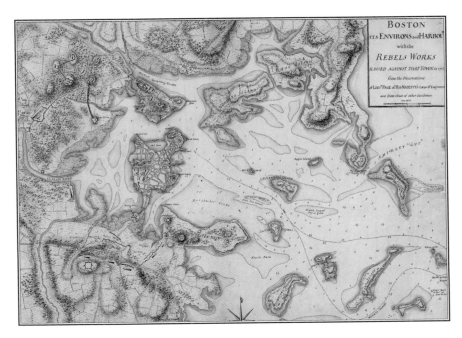

Thomas was living as a wealthy young Englishman and serving in the British army as a commissioned officer in the 1740s. His career in the military would take him to Boston, shown here, where he would play a role in the American Revolution.

contested the election, but the viscount died before it could be settled. Thomas withdrew his contest after his father died.

So far Thomas Gage's military career had gone as he would have expected. But something was happening across the Atlantic Ocean in America that would change many lives, including Thomas's.

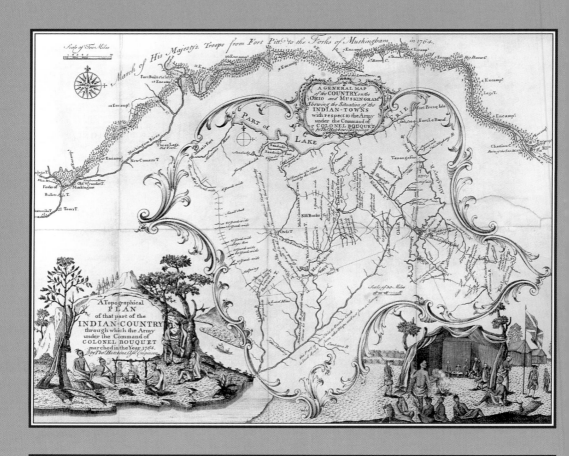

This topographical map shows Ohio and the surrounding areas in colonial times. Thomas was sent to America to fight the French for ownership and control of the area.

2

Off to America

Thomas Gage's regiment, the 44th, was sent to America in 1755. By then Great Britain and France had been fighting each other on and off for more than 50 years. Sometimes they stopped fighting for a few years, but a **truce** never lasted long. In 1755 France controlled Canada and some of the land around the Great Lakes. Great Britain controlled the East coast of America.

The French had built forts along the rivers in the Ohio Valley. Both countries wanted that land. The fighting began when the governor of the Virginia Colony, Robert Dinwiddie, sent a force of men to keep the French from building yet another fort. The triangle of land where the Monongahela and Allegheny Rivers joined to form the Ohio River was where both countries wanted to build a fort.

After a fierce fight, the French ended up with the prized triangle of land. They built Fort Duquesne (pronounced du-kane) there. Governor Dinwiddie immediately sent word to Britain that Virginia needed help. Thomas's regiment, along with the 48th, was ordered to America.

General Edward Braddock commanded Gage's regiment. Braddock's mission was to take Fort Duquesne away from the French and make the French retreat back to Canada. Once the general arrived in America, he met with several colonial governors and other officials to plan the attack. American soldiers, or provincials as they were sometimes called, joined the British soldiers, and they all began the long march to Fort Duquesne. Young

George Washington went along as an aide to General Braddock.

Soon many problems arose. There wasn't enough food, and what they did have was often spoiled. The officers were confused about the plan and sometimes argued. The land was hilly, rocky, and full of trees. The soldiers struggled to get the wagons through. General Braddock was a brave and experienced soldier, but he had never fought in North America. He didn't understand that the French, along with the Indians, who had joined with the French, wouldn't be fighting by the rules he knew.

In Europe, where General Braddock had commanded before, the soldiers fought differently than in North America. The armies lined up in straight lines of soldiers on flat fields. They marched toward each other until the commander told them to stop and shoot. The army whose remaining soldiers backed up or retreated first was the loser. The armies did not

European soldiers stood in straight lines on the battle-field, as shown here in this reenactment. They then marched toward the enemy line until they were told to stop and shoot.

fight in the winter and thought one big battle every other year was enough.

The Braddock expedition marched steadily

along narrow paths and trails with the drummer and fife players noisily announcing the soldiers' presence. At last the army was only 10 miles from Fort Duquesne. There was still no sign of the enemy.

Lieutenant Colonel Gage was sent ahead with an advance guard. He sent word to Braddock that tracks showed the French had recently been

Thomas Gage and George Washington became friends when they served under General Braddock in the battle for Fort Duquesne. They both received praise for the brave way they fought in that battle. A few months later Gage gave a job to one of Washington's friends. The two men wrote letters to each other for several years. In 1757 Gage wrote to Washington that he was glad that his friend was in good health. Many years later the two friends became enemies in the American Revolution.

at the river's edge. Thomas led a force of scouts and 300 British soldiers. Behind him came a working party, which was clearing the way for the main force of soldiers led by Braddock.

As Thomas's advance guard pushed into an open area near the fort, there was a loud whooping. Bullets whizzed by his men. The enemy seemed invisible, as the French and their American Indian allies shot from behind trees and rocks. Thomas's troops fell back and stopped as their leader lined them up to fire on the dim figures in the dark woods. The intense firing scattered the French at first. If Thomas's forces had pressed ahead, they might have chased the attackers away.

Thomas followed the rules instead. His soldiers fell back and reformed their straight lines to fire again. But when they fell back, they ran into the working party coming behind them. Thomas's soldiers fired again. Meanwhile, the French and Indians moved quickly to surround the advance guard and the working party on three sides.

In the confusion the main part of the army led by General Braddock came from behind. The enemy fired from all three sides. Braddock's army was a confusing combination of wagons, horses, and soldiers who fired wildly at the surrounding woods.

George Washington was an aide to British General Edward Braddock before the American Revolution. Thomas and George fought together with Braddock against the French and the Native Americans for control of Fort Duquesne.

It is said that General Braddock called some of his men **cowards** when they tried to take cover and fire from behind trees. The

British soldiers and American volunteers stood bravely but could not win against an enemy they could not see.

F ife players and drummers were important members of the British Army regiments during the American Revolution. The beat of the drum set the pace during long marches, and the fife announced the presence of the king's soldiers. Colonel Francis Smith was the commander of the march to Concord. He rode behind the advance unit who fought on Lexington Green. When he came from the rear and found the soldiers at Lexington in confusion, he called for a drummer. The drummer beat to arms, and the soldiers quickly scrambled into formation as they had been trained.

At last the army began to retreat. General Braddock was seriously wounded. His aide, George Washington, had the general loaded into a wagon and hauled away. Thomas was slightly wounded but organized a rear guard of men to protect the retreating army. Luck was on his side that day because the French and the American Indians did not follow the army to attack again.

General Braddock died a few days later as the defeated army traveled back to Fort Cumberland. Several hundred of his men also died in the battle. Officials in

News of General Braddock's retreat from the battle for Fort Duquesne was not well received in England. Braddock and several hundred men died in the fight.

Britain and America blamed the general for the disastrous outcome. Of course he was just following the rules of war that he knew best.

Thomas went north with his regiment.

When Thomas was in Albany, New York, he led his men north to Canada on several missions. The war that had started in the Ohio country was now called the French and Indian War, also called the Seven Years' War. The battles were often fought in the cold wilderness of Canada.

Thomas came up with an idea during this time. He thought that the British Army should have some soldiers who fought more like the French and their American Indian allies. He offered to lead a new regiment of light-armed **infantry**. These soldiers would be trained in forest fighting. They could move quickly yet still be disciplined soldiers.

Thomas's boss, Commander in Chief John Loudoun, thought it was a good idea. He told Thomas to go ahead and recruit some men. It was near Christmas 1757 when Thomas set up a recruiting headquarters in Brunswick, New Jersey. He probably chose this small village because it was near the home of some American friends named Kemble. One of the sons of the family, Stephen, was an ensign in Thomas's regiment. But it is likely that Thomas really wanted to visit Stephen's sister Margaret.

Margaret was about 24 years old then and known for her beauty and charm. It was easy for Thomas to fall in love with the popular young woman. They made plans to marry in the fall. All too soon he had to return to Albany.

The war began again in the spring. The British lost the Battle of Ticonderoga, in New York, where Thomas commanded part of the advance guard. He was wounded again but not seriously. Finally the British had a victory when they took Fort Duquesne and Fort Frontenac.

The end of 1758 was an exciting time for Thomas. His wedding to Margaret was to be on December 8. Right before the big day he got word that he had been promoted to brigadier general, and the newlyweds moved to Albany early in the new year. General Gage would be in charge of Albany and the forts in that area.

There were more campaigns against the French in Canada until the French finally surrendered in 1760. The Seven Years' War would not officially end until 1763, but Britain maintained control of Canada. Thomas was made the military governor of Montreal.

The general was a good governor. He was fair and able to get along with the defeated Canadians. Thomas made rules about citizens helping put out fires and not letting pigs wander about the town. He ordered that the citizens keep a path shoveled free of snow in front of their houses. Wagons, sleighs, and horseback riders were forbidden to go too fast in town.

One problem for Thomas and his wife was the dull social life in Montreal. Although there were other officers and wives to visit, Montreal was not at all like Albany or New York City. The Gages missed the excitement of life in a city.

In 1761 Thomas was promoted to major general. But it wasn't until October of 1763 that Thomas received word that he had been made the temporary commander in chief of the British forces in North America. A year later his position became permanent.

The Gages packed up their belongings and eagerly made their way back to New York.

Native Americans agreed to stop attacking the British and their army posts after Thomas scored a victory against them in Ohio.

3

Commander in Chief

The new commander in chief of military forces in North America had to find some way to keep the northern Native American tribes from causing trouble. The previous commander in chief, Sir Jeffrey Amherst, had done little to keep the Indians happy. Just before Amherst left for Britain, an Indian **uprising** began.

The Native Americans had never liked the British. Unlike the French, who were traders and trappers, the British wanted to start settlements. The Indians were afraid that the settlers would go farther and farther west into Indian territory. If the French were gone, there would be nothing to stop the British from doing just that.

The Native Americans fought back. They attacked farms and villages and small military outposts. The worst of the uprising took place between Lake Superior and the Ohio River. The Indians burned, killed, and took hundreds of captives.

General Gage had to stop the killing and then find ways to keep the Indians satisfied. In the fall of 1764 he sent soldiers in different directions to trap the worst of the Indians in the middle. The Indians could soon see that the force of soldiers was too big for them to defeat, so they surrendered. Thomas assigned the talks about terms of peace to Sir William Johnson.

Johnson was the Indian superintendent in charge of American Indian affairs for the British government. The Indians trusted him, and all tribes eventually smoked the **peace pipe**. There were a few minor incidents in 1765, but the uprising was over. Thomas Gage had scored his first victory as commander in chief.

Thomas had another important duty besides managing the Indians. He was in charge of all the soldiers in North America. About 5,000 soldiers were spread over the whole eastern half of North America. Thomas had to be sure that each soldier was fed, clothed, and paid. If they were sick, medical care had to be provided. Ministers, or chaplains, as they were called in the army, had to be supervised.

One of the hardest duties was arranging for the regiments of soldiers to be rotated back to Britain. Each regiment spent a certain amount of time in America and then went home to England. Different regiments were then sent to America. It was a complicated process. Sometimes the officers brought their wives and children with them. Everyone had to have a place to live.

Another of Thomas's responsibilities was to the British government. It took a lot of time to do all his paperwork. In Britain the government leaders argued about how the American colonies should be run. They sent many letters to Thomas asking him questions and telling him what to do.

Life wasn't all work for Thomas Gage. He and his wife Margaret lived comfortably in a large house on Broad Street in New York City. The house was surrounded by gardens where their children could play. By the spring of 1763, the Gages had three children, and more would follow.

The Gages had many parties at their home. They attended the theater and went to tea parties and balls. They met famous visitors to New York. As the highest-ranking British officer in North America, Thomas had much power. Even so, he was well liked by his soldiers and the Americans in New York. He was known to be kindhearted and modest. Although some critics questioned his military ability, everyone knew him to be a decent man.

Thomas may have been respected in the colonies, but he was still British, and many Americans disliked the British. The biggest **conflicts** between the colonies and Great Britain were always about money. Great Britain had to spend a lot of money to keep the soldiers in America. The British Parliament thought that

Thomas was a well-known, decent, and respected man in the colonies. Here he is seem greeting a group of children at his home.

the colonies should help pay those costs.

While Thomas was commander in chief, Parliament kept coming up with new ways to make the colonies pay taxes. The colonies already had to provide housing and some food for the British soldiers. In 1765 Parliament voted for new taxes. The one that caused the most uproar in the colonies was called the Stamp Act.

The Stamp Act required that colonists buy

stamps to be placed on certain legal papers, news-papers, and playing cards. Collectors appointed by the British would sell the stamps, thereby generating income for Britain.

This idea did not please the colonists. There were angry town meetings. The famous words, "We shall have no taxation without representation," were first spoken by the colonists at this time. This meant that they did not intend to pay taxes to Britain when the colonies did not have any representatives in Parliament.

In Boston in August 1765 a mob attacked the house of Andrew Oliver, who had been appointed as a stamp agent. They broke windows and destroyed furniture. Finally, Mr. Oliver said he would quit his new job. The same kind of violence happened in many towns all over the colonies before the Stamp Act even went into effect.

General Gage did all he could to stop the attacks. He tried to protect the first shipments of stamps when they arrived. A riot broke out in New York while the stamps were stored at Fort

George. Some angry colonists tried to attack the fort. The officers kept their men quiet inside the fort. After a long night the rioters went home with no harm done to anyone.

The winter of 1765-1766 was a trying one for Thomas and the other British officials. The Stamp Act was not being enforced, but the colonists still seemed ready to fight at any moment. Finally, in May 1766, word came from Britain that the Stamp Act had been **repealed**.

Everyone was relieved. Many colonists thought that the worst of the troubles with Britain was over.

American colonies had used the militia system for 150 years before the Revolution began. Men between 16 and 60 years of age had to own a musket and serve in their town's militia. In March 1775 there were three different companies in each Massachusetts town. There was a regular militia unit, a minutemen company, and an alarm company. Minutemen were ready to move out on very short notice, while the alarm company had older men and was to be used as a last resort. All companies were needed to fight at Lexington and Concord.

There were others who knew that the troubles were just starting.

The American colonists disliked Great Britain's King George III and the Parliament because of the laws and taxes they imposed.

4

Governor Gage

The next few years were restless ones for the colonies. There were already laws made by the British Parliament to control trade and navigation. Few of these laws had ever been enforced. After the Stamp Act was repealed, Parliament tried to enforce the other laws. Sometimes members of Parliament made new laws because they were still trying to raise money to pay for the army in America.

One of the new laws in 1767 was called the Townshend Acts. These acts put taxes on lead, certain kinds of glass and paper, and tea that the colonies bought from Britain. Massachusetts always seemed to be the colony shouting the loudest against Great Britain over the taxes. This time was no exception. The capital of Massachusetts was Boston. That city was the center of all the colonies' most organized efforts to resist Parliament and the British king, George III.

Boston Patriots worked hard to write **pamphlets** and newspaper articles saying how wrong the British government was to tax the colonies. They gave speeches at frequent town meetings. The shopkeepers and other merchants organized into groups that refused to buy any goods shipped from Britain.

By the summer of 1768 Boston seemed like it was about to erupt. There were several small riots and other disagreements between the officials collecting the fees and the colonists. Finally, General Gage was ordered to send soldiers to Boston to keep the peace. In

September two regiments of soldiers arrived by ship in Boston Harbor.

There was no real fighting, but there was plenty of trouble. The residents of Boston did everything they could to make life hard for the British soldiers. The local constables or police often arrested the soldiers for breaking the peace. The citizens constantly hurled insults at the soldiers. If it was winter, the soldiers were pelted with snowballs. If it was spring, the people threw mud, and summer brought stones. And all the time the soldiers were spat upon.

Thomas sent strict orders from his headquarters in New York that the soldiers try to get along with the townspeople. It certainly was not easy. Some of the Boston **Patriot** leaders printed a newspaper called *Journal of the Times.* It contained news from Boston. Although some of the news was true, much of it was made up. Often the paper attacked the British soldiers. It printed many stories saying that the soldiers had committed crimes such as assault and stealing. The newspaper helped stir up the citizens against the British.

Boston residents were boiling over with resentment against Great Britain and its soldiers in the spring of 1770. On the evening of March 5th, townspeople and soldiers roamed the streets yelling at each other and sometimes fighting. Trouble began when a small mob of people threw things at a British soldier. The soldier was standing guard in front of an official building. He was afraid for his life and called for help.

Eight soldiers came to help and faced the mob on the steps of the building. The mob had grown to 50 or 60 people and refused to leave. Some members of the mob hit the soldiers with sticks or clubs while they insulted the soldiers. In the confusion, a soldier fired his **musket** at the mob. The others then fired, too. Five colonists were

The Boston Massacre occurred on March 5, 1770. Five colonists died in the confrontation with British soldiers. The colonists in Boston were tired of British rule and taxes and tension between soldiers and colonists reached a peak. This engraving was produced by Paul Revere.

killed, and several others were wounded.

This event was called the Boston Massacre. The officer in charge quickly sent his men back to the barracks, but it was too late. Word spread and thousands of citizens filled the streets. After a while, Governor Hutchison was finally able to calm the crowd. But the next day, men from the surrounding countryside poured into Boston.

After many discussions, the British commander agreed to take the troops out of Boston to nearby Castle Island. The Americans returned to their homes for the time being.

By the fall of 1770 things had settled down in Boston and in all the American colonies. Many of the colonists seemed to be tired of all the arguments. They just wanted life to go back to normal. But the Patriot leaders still wrote and gave speeches about getting rid of British control.

By October 1772, Thomas was ready for a vacation. The army called it a leave of absence. He took his family back to Britain, saying that business concerning his family in Britain was the reason for the trip.

It was eight months before the Gages left for Britain. There was much to be arranged, but they finally departed on June 8. Many important people in New York liked Thomas. To show their feelings, a dinner was held to honor the general right before he left. The speeches given that night showed that the townspeople of New York thought Thomas was a wise and honorable man.

The Gages reached London on July 8, 1773. The general met with several officials but also did some sightseeing with friends and his brother-in-law, Stephen Kemble, who had come to Britain with the Gages. They also visited Thomas's brother. Margaret Gage had another baby in August. The baby girl was named Charlotte Margaret.

The visit proceeded uneventfully as the Gages visited Highmeadow and made a short trip to Bath. They stayed in London during most of the winter and spring. There were signs that trouble was coming in the colonies again. At the end of January 1774 news came to London of the Boston Tea Party.

The Townshend Acts had been repealed except for the **import tax** on tea. For several years, many of the merchants in the colonies had refused to buy any tea from Britain. What tea they purchased was generally smuggled from Holland. Parliament came up with a plan to help the British tea companies. By changing the way the merchants paid taxes, the Parliament tried to force the Americans to buy British tea instead of Dutch tea.

As might be expected, this news had caused a stir in Boston. On December 16, 1773, Boston **radicals** held their now famous tea party. The colonists dressed as American Indians and boarded a British ship in the harbor. The angry colonists dumped tea overboard. Later some of the colonists were sorry that they had destroyed private property, but the damage had already been done.

The Road to Lexington and Concord

General Gage was determined to make Boston obey the new laws that Parliament had declared. Boston Harbor was to be closed until the colonists paid for the destroyed tea. This news reached Boston before Thomas did. The colonists thought that England was again trying to control them. A few citizens proposed that Boston should pay for the tea. Many town meetings were held to talk about this proposal. In the end the answer was "no."

Thomas landed in Boston in the middle of May 1774. He was welcomed courteously as the new governor of Massachusetts. After he took his **oath** of office, the city held a great banquet in his honor. There were many citizens in Boston who still strongly supported King George III. They were called Loyalists or Tories and most likely they filled many of the seats at the banquet.

June 1 was the date set for the Port Act to begin. Thomas immediately arranged for Boston Harbor to be closed. British Navy ships kept any other ships from entering the harbor. Business activity in Boston soon slowed down. Many men lost their jobs. In spite of this, there was still plenty of food for the local colonists. Towns and villages all over the colonies sent food supplies to Boston.

Meanwhile, Parliament had been hard at work passing more laws. These laws together with the Port Act were called the Intolerable Acts. Members of the council of the colony now were to be chosen by the king. The governor alone would choose judges and sheriffs. Members of a jury were to be chosen by the sheriff. The citizens of the colonies had done all of these jobs themselves in the past.

There's little doubt that Thomas approved of the Intolerable Acts. He had said before that the colonies should not have so much power in governing themselves. Even so, he knew it would be difficult to enforce the laws.

The colonists fought back against the new laws. Some of them organized to stop buying any British goods at all. They got into many arguments among themselves as the organizations tried to enforce the **boycott**. There were also the usual clashes between the British soldiers and Boston citizens.

Thomas had moved the state government to Salem as ordered. He gave the oath of office to some of the new royal councilors on August 8. A date was set for the General Court to meet. Thomas didn't get much more work done. Throughout Massachusetts the citizens refused to obey the new laws. They threatened the new councilors and kept the courts from opening. Men called to serve on juries refused to come. By the end of August people all over Massachusetts began to gather guns and other arms.

It was a dangerous situation, and Thomas moved back to Boston. He had made no plans yet to fight the colonists because he always waited for orders from Britain before acting. But he began to think that some sort of fight could not be avoided.

On September 1, Thomas sent 250 soldiers to Cambridge, a town near Boston, to get 125 barrels of gunpowder, which were stored there. This powder belonged to the colony, and Thomas had the legal right to remove it. He wanted to keep it out of the hands of the radicals.

The entire colony was upset by this action. The countrymen thought that the British had begun an attack. Armed men poured in from all over the countryside. By the next morning, thousands of men had gathered around Boston. Thomas kept his men in Boston, and the colonists finally went home.

So many armed men gathering so quickly must have been a surprising sight for Thomas. While he always knew that the Americans could fight hard, he did not think they were organized enough to do much harm. He thought they lacked good leaders. Soon after this event he wrote to a friend in Britain that 20,000 troops might be needed to suppress the Americans.

Thomas's official letters to Parliament said the government must decide what to do. If they wanted him to march into the countryside, he needed many more soldiers. This was when the British government began to doubt that Thomas was the right man for the job. They could not imagine that the American militias were any match for the King's soldiers. To the British officials, Americans were troublemaking country people. They sent a few reinforcements but not the thousands that Thomas had requested.

Autumn and winter passed with some kind of trouble in Boston almost every day. Most of the time it was arguments and fights between the soldiers and the citizens. The general tried his best to control the British soldiers. He tried so hard to control them that they began to dislike him. They thought he was more concerned about the colonists than his own men.

Soldiers deserted from the British army at an alarming rate during the winter of 1775. The colonists helped create that problem. They often tried to talk the soldiers into leaving the army and being Americans. With the cold, wet winter that seemed to last forever and little food, desertion sounded appealing to many British soldiers.

In spite of not having enough food, the soldiers trained daily. They practiced their shooting skills by firing at a target on a small boat that bobbed in the harbor. The biggest advantage the colonists had, besides their numbers, was their skill at shooting. Thomas hoped some target practice might improve his own soldiers' shooting skills.

By early spring it was easy to see that Thomas was planning some sort of action. The soldiers repaired their tents, mended their camp kettles, and prepared their field equipment. They took short marches through the countryside west of Boston.

Both the Americans and the British had spy networks. Some of the British spies were known Loyalists but at least one man, Dr. Benjamin Church, was an American who only pretended to support the colonial cause. He was able to give many important secrets to Thomas.

The Americans used ordinary citizens to report the activities of the British soldiers. They observed what the soldiers were doing and sometimes listened in as the soldiers talked to each other. American relatives of the

This man is dressed as a minuteman from colonial America. These patriots were called minutemen because they were ready to fight the British at a minute's notice.

soldiers may also have been an important source of information.

Thomas was still waiting for orders from

Britain. Only then would he make a move. At the same time, the colonists were busy training their militias and collecting arms and ammunition. They began moving gunpowder and arms from central locations to hide them.

On April 14, 1775, a secret letter arrived with orders for Thomas. The letter told him to take action against the rebel colonists. The exact way he would do this was left to him, but British officials did want him to arrest the radical leaders.

Thomas decided that the best plan was to march to the nearby town of Concord and destroy the military equipment and powder that was stored there. He picked about 700 of his best men from all regiments and excused them from regular duties. He had already ordered the ships in the harbor to get their **longboats** ready to transport troops across the bay.

The Patriots in Boston were sure that something was going to happen on the night of

Patriots were called to arms on the night of April 18, 1775. They were being warned that the British were marching toward Lexington and Concord, Massachusetts.

April 18. They did not know if the British would travel by land across the Boston Neck or by boat to a landing point on the mainland.

The Patriot leaders planned several different ways to spread the news out of Boston. They hoped that at least one way would be successful.

About 10 o'clock on the evening of the 18th, Thomas gave the order for the troops to move out. Thomas was a cautious man. He probably knew that his actions could be the beginning of a long struggle.

Paul Revere is shown here in his famous ride toward Lexington at about midnight on April 18, 1775.

Revolution!

Even before the longboats hit the water, the Patriots were on the road to warn the Patriots of Concord. The spy network was hard at work, and by late afternoon it had reported to the Patriot leaders that something was planned for that night. One of the leaders, Dr. Joseph Warren, sent a message to a secret informer. That informer confirmed that the British were on the way to Concord. Dr. Warren sent for another Patriot, Paul Revere. He told the silversmith to hurry to Lexington to warn the rebel leaders, John Hancock and Samuel Adams. The pair was known to be staying in that area.

Paul Revere first sent a signal to Charlestown across

the Charles River that the British were coming by water. It had been arranged that two men would go up into the steeple of the Old North Church and light one lantern if the British were coming by land and two lanterns if by water. Patriots across the river in Charlestown were watching. When the light of two lanterns twinkled through the night, a rider was immediately sent toward Concord.

Paul Revere went to the north part of Boston, where he had hidden a small boat. Two friends rowed him across to the ferry landing at Charlestown. Other Patriots met him there and gave him a horse. In minutes he was riding swiftly on the dark road to Concord.

Another rider, William Dawes, had left by land over the Boston neck. He took a different route to Concord. By sending several messengers, the Patriots hoped that at least one would get through to warn Adams and Hancock.

Back in Boston the soldiers had been rowed from the west side of Boston across the Back Bay to land at Lechmere Point. It was midnight

Samuel Adams was a strong leader in the
patriot's movement for independence from
Britain. He formed the Boston chapter of the
Sons of Liberty and was behind many of the
protest against British rule. He was one of the
signers of the Declaration of Independence.

before all of the men could be rowed across the
Charles River. They waded north across creeks
and through swampy ground before they could
get on the road to Lexington.

John Hancock was a businessman who worked closely with Samuel Adams in demanding the removal of British troops from Boston. Hancock was the presiding officer of the Continental Congress at the time the Declaration of Independence was signed, as such his is the first signature on the document.

Paul Revere had to make several changes to his route on his way to Lexington. British soldiers patrolled the road, but he managed to avoid them at first. The patrols had no idea that several hundred of their fellow soldiers were marching toward Concord.

By midnight Revere reached Lexington and the house where John Hancock and Samuel Adams were staying. On his way he had spread the word of the army that approached. He rode on toward Concord after warning the Patriot leaders and rousing the Lexington militia.

Several hours later the British soldiers reached Lexington. The Lexington militia was lined up on the village green. The British redcoats marched in several groups. Two of the groups in front marched straight at the militia. The men stared at each other. Their leaders had warned both the militia and the redcoats not to fire first. Finally someone did fire. The British soldiers began firing,

When Paul Revere was rowed up to the Charlestown ferry landing to begin his famous ride, there was a horse waiting for him. According to tradition the horse was named Brown Beauty. She was a New England saddlehorse—big, strong, and very fast. Brown Beauty's long strides helped Revere escape from a British patrol on the Lexington Road. Later, when Revere was captured near Concord and then released, Beauty was given to a British sergeant. The soldier rode Brown Beauty off into the night. Revere never saw her again.

The British were met at Lexington by the colonial minutemen. The shots fired at Lexington on April 19, 1775, started the Revolutionary War.

and the militia fell back. By the time the smoke cleared, 8 of the 60 or so militiamen were dead and several others were seriously wounded. Only one of the British soldiers was wounded. It has never been determined which side fired the first shot. It may have been accidental. In later years it was called "the shot heard 'round the world." It was April 19, 1775, and the American Revolution had begun.

The British never made any serious search for Samuel Adams or John Hancock. It is not known for sure why Thomas decided not to follow that part of his orders. He may have realized that it would not have stopped the Americans if he arrested those two leaders. Thomas knew that there were many other leaders to take their place.

The British marched on to Concord and did what they had been sent to do. They destroyed any military equipment that hadn't been hidden by the colonists. The fight with the militias was different at Concord. The local militia companies had begun to pour into Concord. To the complete surprise of the British officers, these American soldiers were organized and fearless. More than anything else, the Americans were deadly accurate marksmen.

After a battle at Concord's North Bridge, the British began a hasty retreat the way they had come. By now the militia outnumbered the British. The Americans made a huge moving circle around the

On the night of April 18, 1775, Thomas ordered 700 soldiers to march to Concord and capture or destroy the patriot's supplies. The soldiers were met the next day by a militia skilled in the use and rifles and determined to fight. Once surrounded, the British soldiers were forced to retreat.

British as the redcoats marched in formation. The militia ambushed the British from every side. The road ran through tree-covered hills with many stone walls. The British soldiers were shot one by one.

Earlier Thomas had received word that his forces needed reinforcements. These troops arrived just in time. The tired soldiers who had marched to Concord and halfway back cheered when they heard the drums of the new units. Probably the reinforcements kept the British from having a total defeat. The Americans fought the rear of the British brigade all the way to Charlestown.

It was dark before the British forces were safe at last on the high ground above Charlestown. The exhausted men sank onto the damp ground and slept. Later that night they rowed across the river to Boston.

The militia stayed beyond the reach of the guns of the British ships in the harbor. Fifty Americans died that day or later from their wounds. Almost 90 British soldiers died or were reported missing.

Thomas and the other commanders had seriously underestimated the colonists' numbers and determination. He had hoped that the Patriot militias would see the British soldiers and know that it was hopeless to fight. Instead the battles at Lexington and Concord had brought the colonies together. The cause was now clear. They were fighting for their land and homes and families.

At the beginning of June, Thomas still hoped that

the two sides could reach a peaceful agreement, but a truce was never reached. Thomas ordered his soldiers to improve the fortifications, which he hoped would keep the Americans from seriously planning an attack. By the middle of June, Thomas had given up on any peace with the colonies. He decided to take action to clear the Patriot forces from the Charlestown Peninsula on the north and Dorchester Heights on the southeast side of Boston.

On the evening of June 16, noises coming from the Charlestown Peninsula made Thomas think that the Americans were digging in on the hills. One of the other commanders said that the British should attack immediately before the Americans could finish their fortifications. This would have been a good plan if the general and his officers hadn't taken too much time deciding.

The attack on Bunker Hill didn't start until the afternoon of June 17, 1775. The British troops landed on the end of the Charlestown Peninsula and began a frontal assault on the American positions first on Breed's Hill and then on Bunker

The Battle of Bunker Hill took place on June 17, 1775, in Charlestown. Thomas organized the British assault. Although the British won the battle, the patriots fought bravely and caused many losses amongst the British army.

Hill. The Americans shot from their trenches. It was a bloody battle, as one after another British soldiers fell to the skilled Patriot shooters.

Eventually the British did manage to push the Americans back and take the two hills, but they suffered terrible losses. Thomas later reported 226 killed and 828 wounded. American losses were fewer at 115 killed and 271 wounded.

Thomas canceled the planned attack on Dorchester Heights. He decided that he did not have enough men to undertake that mission.

On June 25 Thomas wrote to his superiors in London. He said that he thought the attack on the two hills was necessary but was sorry that the losses were so high. It is likely the general expected that orders for him to return to Britain would soon come.

He was right. In September he was asked to return to London to help plan the next year's operations. It was the king's way of being easy on the general. He sailed for Britain on October 11, 1775, but the Revolution continued for another six years.

It was a difficult time for Thomas. Many men in the British government blamed Thomas for not putting an end to the American rebellion. But life went on for the general and his family. He did some military work over the years, including training some troops in 1781. He retained the title of governor of Massachusetts throughout the war and received a salary for that position. He was made a full general in 1782. But his military career had really ended on the day he boarded the ship for Britain in 1775.

After an illness Thomas died at his home in Portland Place on April 2, 1787. He was buried at Firle, the Gage family home, with his ancestors. Mrs. Gage lived for almost 37 more years and died on February 9, 1824, at the age of 90.

There seems no doubt that General Thomas Gage was an honorable man. He was not in favor of war and always tried to settle disputes peaceably. He was a respected governor, who

Historians have said that General Gage's American wife, Margaret, was the informer who told Dr. Joseph Warren of the British plan to take Concord. She made no secret of her distress that her husband was on the opposite side from her countrymen. The lands that she and her husband owned in America were not taken from them during the war. Some say this is proof that she was rewarded for helping the Americans. But the fact that the couple stayed together until death makes it seem unlikely that Mrs. Gage betrayed her husband's trust.

was able to improve the lives of the people he governed. His worst mistake may have been not recognizing that the Americans' hearts cried out for freedom, and nothing less would do.

GLOSSARY

borough—an area or town that has a representative in Parliament.

boycott—to refuse to buy or use certain goods.

conflict—disagreement or fight.

coward—a person who lacks courage in facing danger.

import tax—a tax on goods brought from a foreign country.

infantry—soldiers who fight on foot.

longboat—a large rowboat carried onboard a sailing ship

musket—a heavy gun first used in the 1500s; similar to the rifle.

oath—a promise to do something.

pamphlet—a short, unbound booklet.

Patriot—a colonist who supported America but not Britain.

peace pipe—a long tobacco pipe smoked by Indians as a token of peace.

radical—a colonial leader who wanted to make the British leave America.

regiment—a unit of infantry soldiers.

repeal—to take back or withdraw; usually a law or tax.

treason—the crime of helping the enemy instead of your own country.

truce—an agreement to stop fighting for a period of time.

uprising—a revolt or breaking away from the official authorities.

CHRONOLOGY

1719–20	Thomas Gage is born in England around this time.
1728	Attends school at Westminster.
1740	Gage had entered the army by this time.
1741	Purchases a commission as lieutenant and then a captain in 1743.
1744	Fights the French at Flanders in Belgium.
1755	Sent to America to fight French and Indians.
1758	Marries Margaret Kemble, an American, on December 8.
1760	Appointed military governor of Montreal in Canada.
1761	Promoted to major general.
1763	Becomes commander in chief of British forces in North America; moves to New York.
1773	Travels to Britain on a leave of absence from the army.
1774	Returns to America as governor of Massachusetts after the Boston Tea Party.
1775	Orders march to Concord that starts the Revolutionary War; plans and carries out the Battle of Bunker Hill; is recalled to Britain.
1787	After an illness, dies on April 2.

REVOLUTIONARY WAR TIME LINE ═══

1765   The Stamp Act is passed by the British. Violent protests against it break out in the colonies.

1766   Britain ends the Stamp Act.

1767   Britain passes a law that taxes glass, painter's lead, paper, and tea in the colonies.

1770   Five colonists are killed by British soldiers in the Boston Massacre.

1773   People are angry about the taxes on tea. They throw boxes of tea from ships in Boston harbor into the water. It ruins the tea. The event is called the Boston Tea Party.

1774   The British pass laws to punish Boston for the Boston Tea Party. They close Boston harbor. Leaders in the colonies meet to plan a response to these actions.

1775   The battles of Lexington and Concord begin the American Revolution.

1776   The Declaration of Independence is signed. France and Spain give money to help the Americans fight Britain. Nathan Hale is captured by the British. He is charged with being a spy and is executed.

1777   Leaders choose a flag for America. The American troops win some important battles over the British. General Washington and his troops spend a very cold, hungry winter in Valley Forge.

1778   France sends ships to help the Americans win the war. The British are forced to leave Philadelphia.

1779	French ships head back to France. The French support the Americans in other ways.
1780	Americans discover that Benedict Arnold is a traitor. He escapes to the British. Major battles take place in North and South Carolina.
1781	The British surrender at Yorktown.
1783	A peace treaty is signed in France. British troops leave New York.
1787	The U.S. Constitution is written. Delaware becomes the first state in the Union.
1789	George Washington becomes the first president. John Adams is vice president.

FURTHER READING

Edmonds, Walter. *The Matchlock Gun*. New York: Putnam, 1989.

Egger-Bovet, Howard, and Marlene Smith-Baranzini. *US Kids History: Book of the American Revolution*. Boston: Little, Brown, 1994.

Grote, JoAnn A. *Paul Revere: American Patriot*. Philadelphia: Chelsea House, 2000.

Hull, Mary. *Boston Tea Party*. Springfield, NJ: Enslow, 1999.

Maestro, Betsy, and Giulio Maestro. *Struggle for a Continent: The French and Indian Wars 1689-1763*. New York: HarperCollins, 2000.

Moore, Kay. *If You Lived at the Time of the American Revolution*. New York: Scholastic, 1997.

Murphy, Jim. *A Young Patriot: The American Revolution as Experienced by One Boy*. New York: Clarion Books, 1996.

PICTURE CREDITS

INDEX

Adams, Samuel, 61, 62, 65, 67
Albemarle, Duke of, 12
Amherst, Jeffrey, 29

Boston Harbor, closing of, 46, 49, 50
Boston Massacre, 40-42
Boston Tea Party, 44-46, 49
Braddock, Edward, 16-23
Bunker Hill, Battle of, 70-72

Church, Benjamin, 55
Concord
    Battle of, 67-69
    British march to, 57-59, 61-65
    Revere's ride to, 61-65
Culloden, Battle of, 11-12

Dawes, William, 62
Dinwiddie, Robert, 15-16
Duquesne, Fort, 16-22, 25

Fontenoy, Battle of, 11
French and Indian War, 15-26
Frontenac, Fort, 25

Gage, Thomas
    in Albany, 25
    in army, 10-12
    birth of, 8
    as brigadier general, 25
    in Britain on leave from army,
        42-44, 46
    in Canada, 26-27
    children of, 32, 43
    as commander in chief of British
        troops in America, 26-27,
        29-35, 37-42, 46-47, 49-59
    death of, 73
    education of, 9
    family of, 7-9, 10, 43
    and fighting French at Flanders, 11
    and fighting Scottish at Culloden,
        11-12
    as general, 72

    as governor of Massachusetts, 46-47,
        49-59, 64-72, 73
    as major general, 26
    and marriage, 25, 26, 27, 32, 47, 73
    as military governor of Montreal,
        26-27
    in New York, 27, 32, 43
    in politics, 12-13
    and recalled to Britain, 72-73
Gage, Viscount (father), 7-8, 10, 12-13
George, Fort, 34-35
George III, King, 38, 46, 50

Hancock, John, 61, 62, 65, 67
Hutchison, Governor, 42

Intolerable Acts, 50-51

Johnson, William, 30

Kemble, Margaret (wife), 25, 26, 27, 32,
    47, 73

Lexington
    Battle of, 65-67, 69
    Revere's ride to, 61-65
Loudoun, John, 24

Native Americans, 29-31, 46

Oliver, Andrew, 34

Port Act, 50

Revere, Paul, 61-62, 64, 65

Stamp Act, 33-35, 37

Ticonderoga, Battle of, 25
Townshend Acts, 37-38, 44

Warren, Joseph, 61
Washington, George, 17, 22

ABOUT THE AUTHOR

Southwest Missouri writer **BONNIE HINMAN** has had five children's historical novels and three children's biographies published, as well as many articles and stories. She enjoys speaking at schools and reading all kinds of books. Mrs. Hinman lives with her husband, Bill, and her son Brad in Joplin, Missouri, where her daughter Beth and son-in-law Eric also reside.

Senior Consulting Editor **ARTHUR M. SCHLESINGER, JR.** is the leading American historian of our time. He won the Pulitzer Prize for his book *The Age of Jackson* (1945), and again for *A Thousand Days* (1965). This chronicle of the Kennedy Administration also won a National Book Award. He has written many other books, including a multi-volume series, *The Age of Roosevelt.* Professor Schlesinger is the Albert Schweitzer Professor of the Humanities at the City University of New York, and has been involved in several other Chelsea House projects, including the Colonial Leaders series of biographies on the most prominent figures of early American history.